THE REJECTED STONE

"The stone which the builders refused is become the head stone of the corner." —Psalm 118:22 (KJV)

Pastor Dr. Claudine Benjamin

THE REJECTED STONE. Copyright @ 2025. Pastor Dr. Claudine Benjamin. All rights reserved.

For more information or to book an event, contact:
inspiredtowinsouls@gmail.com

No part of this publication may be reproduced, stored in a retrieval system or transmitted in any form or by any means, electronic, mechanical, photocopying, recording or otherwise without the prior written permission of the author.

Published by:

Editor: Cleveland O. McLeish (Author C. Orville McLeish)

ISBN: 978-1-965635-49-0 (paperback)

Unless otherwise stated, all Scripture quotations are taken from the King James Version (KJV).

Scripture quotations marked "KJV" are taken from the Holy Bible, King James Version (Public Domain).

Scripture quotations marked (NIV) are taken from the Holy Bible, New International Version®, NIV®. Copyright © 1973, 1978, 1984 by Biblica, Inc.™ Used by permission of Zondervan. All rights reserved worldwide.

Dedication

To every soul who has ever been overlooked, misunderstood, discarded, or told, *"You are not good enough."*

This book is lovingly dedicated to the rejected stones—those who were dropped, not chosen, falsely accused, or prematurely disqualified. You are the very ones God is raising up in this hour.

To the dreamers whose vision was dismissed.

To the leaders who were pushed out of places they were sent to bless.

To the voices that were silenced because they did not fit the system.

To the anointed who were never appointed by man.

To the warriors who were wounded in the field but still refused to quit.

This is for you.

You are not forgotten. You are not disqualified. You are not useless. You are God's chosen cornerstone in the making. Every "no" you received was making room for God's "yes." Every time they shut you out, God was carving out a foundation for you to stand on.

To my family, my beloved church family at New Life Church Community Ministries, and every stone that has been rejected but kept their integrity—may this message confirm that God never wastes pain. He turns the overlooked into the overcomers and the abandoned into the anointed.

You are not just a stone.
You are the cornerstone.

Acknowledgments

With deep humility and gratitude, I acknowledge the sovereign hand of God—the Master Builder—who has lovingly crafted this message in the depths of my spirit. Without His grace, there would be no story to tell and no stone to recover.

To my Lord and Savior, Jesus Christ—the Cornerstone whom the world rejected but whom the Father exalted—I give all the glory. Thank You for transforming my own rejection into revelation and using my scars as a testimony of Your faithfulness.

To my beloved family, thank you for your unwavering support, love, and prayers. You have been pillars beside me, strengthening me when I was weak and reminding me of who I am when the world tried to make me forget.

To the New Life Church Community Ministries family, your steadfast encouragement and spiritual covering have been a fertile ground for vision to flourish. Thank you for walking this journey with me, praying over every word, and believing in the message God birthed through this book.

To every reader who has ever been overlooked, discarded, misunderstood, or pushed aside—this book is for you. You are seen. You are chosen. You are being set into place by the hand of the Chief Architect Himself. May these pages minister healing, ignite destiny, and confirm what heaven has already spoken over your life.

To every editor, intercessor, friend, and fellow laborer who stood with me behind the scenes—thank you. You have helped lift the message of this work and carried it with integrity and excellence.

And finally, to every builder who refused the stone—thank you. Your rejection made space for God's selection. What you pushed away, He picked up. What you saw as unfit, He saw as foundational. To God be the glory—for the tables turned, the walls rebuilt, and the stones restored.

About the Author

Pastor Dr. Claudine Benjamin is a passionate preacher, anointed teacher, and prophetic author called to reach the rejected, heal the hurting, and awaken the church to its God-given mandate. Known for her bold voice, unwavering faith, and unshakable commitment to truth, she ministers with both power and compassion to those who feel overlooked, forgotten, or cast aside by life and systems.

As a visionary leader, Pastor Claudine has shepherded a thriving and Spirit-led congregation that embraces healing, deliverance, biblical teaching, and outreach with urgency and authenticity. Her leadership reflects the heart of Christ—she leads not from a pedestal but from a place of humility, transparency, and deep intimacy with God.

Pastor Claudine's ministry extends far beyond the pulpit. She is a sought-after speaker, conference host, mentor to emerging leaders, and intercessor with a prophetic edge. Her books are birthed not from theory but from tested fire—real experiences, real rejection, and real revelation. Through each page, she pours out the oil that came from crushing, the wisdom that came from waiting, and the fire that came from enduring seasons of being misunderstood and misjudged.

She is the author of multiple powerful works, including:

- The Urgency in Winning Souls
- How to Handle the Process After the Storm
- Purpose Cannot Die
- Built to Last
- You Have Mastered Survival Mode: It's Now Time to Live
- Christ Is My Firm Foundation

…among others.

With a deep love for scripture and a prophetic burden for the broken, Pastor Claudine writes for the misfit, the dismissed, and the discarded. Her message is consistent and clear: Your rejection was not a curse—it was a setup for your elevation.

Beyond her ministry platform, she is a dedicated mother, mentor, and spiritual mother to many. Her life is a testimony of restoration, her voice a trumpet for truth, and her calling a commission from heaven to raise up living stones who will rebuild ruined places.

Pastor Dr. Claudine Benjamin lives by this unshakable conviction: *"If God can use what man rejected, then I am proof that He builds masterpieces from what others abandon."*

Table of Contents

Dedication iii

Acknowledgments v

About the Author vii

Introduction: Rejected but Not Forgotten 11

Chapter 1: The Builder's Blind Spot 13

Chapter 2: God's Pattern for the Overlooked 17

Chapter 3: Jesus—The Ultimate Rejected Stone 21

Chapter 4: When Rejection Becomes Redirection 25

Chapter 5: From Cast Aside to Cornerstone 29

Chapter 6: Birth Movements 45

Chapter 7: The Process of Becoming Foundational 53

Chapter 8: You Were Rejected for a Reason 61

Chapter 9: The Pain of Rejection and the Purpose Behind It 73

Chapter 10: Favor Finds the Forsaken 77

Chapter 11: When Man Says No, But God Says Yes 81

Chapter 12: The Stone That Broke the Mold 85

Chapter 13: The Anointing That Cannot Be Ignored 89

Chapter 14: Built by God, Not by Man 93

Chapter 15: When You Become What They Needed All Along 97

Chapter 16: Restoration and Reinstatement 101

Chapter 17: A Seat at the Table You Were Shut Out From 105

Chapter 18: Rebuilding With Rejected Stones 109

Chapter 19: Satan's Counterfeit Doors 117

Chapter 20: Maintaining Access Through Worship and Warfare .. 121

Chapter 21: The Door of the Final Hour.. 125

Scripture Reference Index.. 129

Conclusion: From Rejection to Royalty 133

Introduction

Rejected but Not Forgotten

The rejected stone. It's more than just a poetic phrase—it's a prophetic reality that echoes throughout the lives of many. In Psalm 118:22 (KJV), the psalmist writes, **"The stone which the builders refused is become the head stone of the corner."** This verse speaks of the profound transformation of something discarded into something essential. It represents the shift from rejection to elevation, from obscurity to prominence, from being cast away to being placed at the center of God's divine plan.

The greatest fulfillment of this scripture is found in Jesus Christ, who was rejected by the religious leaders and crucified by man—yet was chosen by God to become the Chief Cornerstone of our salvation. But this divine pattern of rejection turning into selection is not limited to Christ alone. It is a model that God still uses today in the lives of His people. Throughout scripture and history, God has consistently chosen the unlikely, the forgotten, the underestimated—the rejected stones—and placed them in foundational positions.

This book is written for those who have been passed over, dismissed, and undervalued. Maybe you were overlooked by family, denied by institutions, or counted out by society. But the rejection of man does not cancel the calling of God. In fact, it often confirms it.

In the chapters ahead, we will explore how rejection can be a setup for divine positioning. We will look at how God uses pain to refine purpose and how what man disqualifies, God sanctifies. You will see how Jesus embodied the rejected stone and how you, too, are being shaped for significance in the kingdom of God.

This book is a declaration: You may have been rejected, but you are not forgotten. God is about to place you where they never thought you'd belong.

Chapter 1

The Builder's Blind Spot

"The stone which the builders refused is become the head stone of the corner." —Psalm 118:22 (KJV)

Builders are expected to have vision—to see potential where others do not. They are supposed to know how to select, measure, and align materials to create something lasting and purposeful. Yet even the most experienced builders can miss a stone that's been chosen by God.

In biblical times, builders would examine stones for flaws. If a stone had a crack, was uneven, or didn't appear strong enough to bear weight, it would be cast aside. It wasn't personal—it was practical. But what if the builder's assessment was limited? What if they couldn't see the strength in what they dismissed?

REJECTION IS OFTEN BASED ON LIMITED VISION

The builders in Psalm 118 represent systems, structures, and leaders who evaluate based on human standards. But God doesn't choose based on outward appearance—He looks at the heart (see 1 Samuel 16:7). The same God who chose a shepherd boy over seasoned warriors, a barren woman over fertile rivals, and a stuttering man over eloquent speakers—is the same God who chooses the rejected stone.

Jesus Himself was born in a manger and raised in Nazareth—a place of no reputation. **"Can anything good come out of Nazareth?"** was a common sentiment (see John 1:46). He didn't look like a Messiah. He didn't sound like a king. So the builders—those in power, those in control—refused Him. But their rejection couldn't stop God's purpose.

MAN'S REFUSAL DOESN'T CANCEL GOD'S SELECTION

God doesn't need man's approval to advance His plan. The builders may reject, but heaven still anoints. David wasn't invited to the anointing ceremony, yet oil still found him. Joseph was thrown in a pit and sold into slavery, yet God made him a prince in Egypt. Moses was exiled from Egypt, yet returned as a deliverer.

What does this mean for you? It means you can stop seeking validation from people who cannot see your value. Their rejection is not the end of your story—it may be the beginning of God's unveiling.

THE HEAD CORNERSTONE IS MEANT TO ALIGN OTHERS

The head cornerstone is the most critical stone in a building. It aligns and supports all other stones. That's what Jesus became, and that's what God is shaping you to be. You may have been rejected because of your uniqueness, your boldness, your truth, your anointing—but those very things are the reasons God chose you.

The stone they rejected is the one that holds the structure together. You are not just any stone—you are a foundational one.

FROM PIT TO PLATFORM

Sometimes, the path to elevation is paved with rejection. Joseph was rejected by his brothers, slandered by Potiphar's wife, and forgotten in prison—but he still arrived at the palace. Why? Because the rejection was never a detour—it was a divine strategy.

What if you stopped asking, *"Why did they reject me?"* and started asking, *"What is God preparing me for?"*

REFLECTION QUESTIONS

1. Who are the "builders" in your life whose rejection wounded you?

2. What qualities have others dismissed that God may be using for your elevation?

3. How can you begin to embrace your identity as a cornerstone rather than a castoff?

Chapter 2

God's Pattern for the Overlooked

"But God hath chosen the foolish things of the world to confound the wise; and God hath chosen the weak things of the world to confound the things which are mighty." —1 Corinthians 1:27 (KJV)

Rejection has a pattern—but so does God's redemption. Throughout scripture, God reveals a divine pattern of selecting those whom others overlook. He doesn't choose based on resumes or reputations. He chooses based on readiness, humility, and the capacity to carry purpose through pain.

DIVINE PREFERENCE FOR THE UNDERVALUED

God has always shown a preference for the least likely. Abel over Cain. Jacob over Esau. David over Eliab. Gideon, the weakest in his clan. Esther, the orphan girl turned queen. Time and again, God bypasses the obvious and chooses the hidden.

Why? Because He delights in showing that power belongs to Him alone. He doesn't need a perfect vessel; He needs a willing one.

Pastor Dr. Claudine Benjamin

BEING OVERLOOKED ISN'T BEING OVERRULED

You may not have been their first choice, but you are still God's plan. Being passed over by man does not eliminate your position in God's timeline. Sometimes the longer the wait, the greater the unveiling.

Samuel almost anointed the wrong king by choosing Eliab, who looked the part. But God stopped him: **"Look not on his countenance…for the Lord seeth not as man seeth" (see 1 Samuel 16:7)**. God had already seen David in the field.

If man's eyes missed you, don't worry—God's eyes were on you the whole time.

REJECTION IS OFTEN A STAGE FOR REVELATION

It's in the place of being forgotten that God often gives the clearest vision. While Joseph was in prison, God revealed dreams. While Moses was in exile, God revealed a burning bush. While David was tending sheep, God sent the prophet. Rejection creates space for divine encounters.

THE WILDERNESS PREPARES THE STONE

The wilderness, like rejection, is not meant to destroy—it's meant to develop. It is in the overlooked seasons that God chisels, shapes, and tests the stone for strength. When the builders finally see what God has done, the stone they once discarded will be irreplaceable.

REFLECTION QUESTIONS

1. In what ways have you seen God use rejection to redirect your life?

2. What strength has grown in you during your season of being overlooked?

3. Can you identify the divine pattern in your personal story?

Chapter 3

Jesus—The Ultimate Rejected Stone

> "He is despised and rejected of men; a man of sorrows, and acquainted with grief..." —Isaiah 53:3 (KJV)

Jesus Christ is the perfect and prophetic fulfillment of the rejected stone. His life mirrors what it means to be misunderstood, marginalized, and ultimately elevated by God.

REJECTED FROM THE BEGINNING

Even before His birth, there was no room for Him in the inn. As a child, His family fled to Egypt to escape Herod's wrath. He grew up in a town no one respected. From the start, Jesus lived the experience of rejection—geographically, politically, and socially.

But none of this diminished His calling. Rejection was written into His redemptive story.

REFUSED BY THE RELIGIOUS

The builders in Psalm 118 were not pagans—they were religious leaders. It was the religious elite who saw Jesus as a threat to their systems. They refused the stone because it didn't fit their mold. He healed on the Sabbath. He spoke with sinners. He overturned their tables. He exposed their hypocrisy.

They rejected Him because He revealed their corruption.

But Jesus was not surprised by their dismissal. In Matthew 21:42, He quoted Psalm 118: **"Did ye never read in the scriptures, the stone which the builders rejected, the same is become the head of the corner?"** He knew who He was, even when they refused to see it.

THE CROSS WAS THE BUILDERS' FINAL REFUSAL

The crucifixion was humanity's loudest "No" to Jesus. They didn't just reject His teaching—they rejected His existence. They beat Him, mocked Him, and nailed Him to a tree. But the cross didn't cancel His purpose; it fulfilled it.

The resurrection was God's final "Yes" in response to man's "No." He rose in power, vindicated by heaven, exalted above all names. The rejected stone had become the cornerstone of a new covenant.

IF JESUS WAS REJECTED, SO WILL YOU BE

To follow Jesus is to walk the same path. **"If the world hate you, ye know that it hated me before it hated you." (John 15:18 - KJV).** If Jesus—pure, perfect, and holy—was despised, you should not be surprised when rejection comes.

But just as He overcame, so will you. Rejection does not define you. It refines you.

YOU ARE BEING FORMED IN HIS IMAGE

To be rejected like Jesus is to be positioned like Jesus. Every time you're passed over, remember—so was He. Every time your motives are misunderstood—so were His. But your story, like His, will not end in the grave. It will end in glory.

You are a living stone, being built into a spiritual house (see 1 Peter 2:5). Rejected stones make the strongest foundations.

REFLECTION QUESTIONS

1. How does Jesus' rejection encourage you in your own?

2. In what areas of life are you experiencing the same pattern of misunderstanding?

3. What does it mean for you to identify with Christ as the rejected stone?

Chapter 4

When Rejection Becomes Redirection

"And we know that all things work together for good to them that love God, to them who are the called according to His purpose." —Romans 8:28 (KJV)

Rejection often feels like a closed door, a painful no, or a silent dismissal. But what if it is not a denial—but a divine detour? What if rejection is the very tool God uses to re-route us into purpose?

God is not the author of confusion, but He is a Master at redirection. Rejection in the hands of man may be cruel, but in the hands of God, it becomes a compass—pointing you away from what you thought you needed toward what He always planned.

DIVINE DETOURS: JOSEPH'S REJECTION WAS A SET-UP

Joseph was sold into slavery by his brothers. They rejected his dreams, his favor, and his voice. He was thrown into a pit, sold to strangers, falsely accused, and forgotten in prison. But every rejection was part of a redirection.

Genesis 50:20 tells us Joseph's own revelation: **"But as for you, ye thought evil against me; but God meant it unto good…"** Joseph's rejection was God's route to the palace. Without the pit, there would have been no position.

Sometimes rejection is not punishment. It's placement.

BEING SHUT OUT CAN BE A SHIELD

When people walk away, doors close, or opportunities slip away, we often see it as failure. But what if God is shielding you? What if He blocked what you wanted to give you what you needed?

God closed the door to the Garden of Eden after Adam sinned—not as punishment alone, but to prevent man from living forever in a fallen state (see Genesis 3:22-24). Rejection became protection.

There are some "No's" from heaven that are actually *"Not here—there's better ahead."*

REDIRECTION IS OFTEN IMMEDIATE, BUT RECOGNITION IS DELAYED

You may not understand why the door closed while you're standing in front of it. It's not until you're further down the road that you look back and realize: God saved you from something.

This is why trust is essential. **"Trust in the LORD with all thine heart; and lean not unto thine own understanding." (Proverbs 3:5 - KJV).** Rejection doesn't make sense in the moment, but it fits in God's masterpiece.

PAUL'S MACEDONIAN CALL: A CLOSED DOOR WITH A GREATER MISSION

In Acts 16:6–10, Paul and his companions tried to go into Asia, but the Holy Spirit forbade them. The door was closed. Then Paul had a vision of a man in Macedonia pleading for help. The rejection of Asia led to the redirection of Macedonia, where God moved powerfully.

This reminds us: God doesn't just call us to places—He also calls us away from places.

GOD REDIRECTS TO REVEAL HIS GREATER GLORY

Every detour in your life has purpose. Every shut door, delayed answer, or sudden dismissal carries the fingerprint of divine redirection. God is not just shifting your location—He's aligning your life with destiny.

REFLECTION QUESTIONS

1. Have you experienced rejection that later proved to be redirection?

2. What might God be protecting or preparing you for right now?

3. How can you embrace divine detours without bitterness?

Chapter 5

From Cast Aside to Cornerstone

"Therefore thus saith the Lord GOD, Behold, I lay in Zion for a foundation a stone, a tried stone, a precious cornerstone, a sure foundation: he that believeth shall not make haste." — **Isaiah 28:16 (KJV)**

One of the most powerful principles in the kingdom of God is transformation. What man casts aside, God often chooses as a cornerstone. In ancient construction, the cornerstone was the most important stone in the building—it determined the entire structure's alignment and strength.

When the builders reject a stone, they presume it has no value. But when God selects a cornerstone, He picks the one that has endured, been tested, and proven trustworthy.

THE CORNERSTONE IS CHOSEN, NOT CHOSEN BY COMMITTEE

God doesn't need a panel to approve His decisions. He doesn't ask for permission from the builders. He selects what He wills based on eternal wisdom.

Jesus was the stone chosen by God before the foundations of the world. Isaiah prophesied that He would be "a tried stone"—tested and proven. This is the same process many believers endure. Before you're placed in a foundational position, you must first be tried.

Rejection is part of your training. Pain is part of your preparation.

THE PROCESS OF BECOMING A CORNERSTONE

Before a stone can bear weight, it must be shaped. That means cutting, striking, and smoothing. Many believers cry out for elevation but resist the chiseling. But the process cannot be skipped. God prepares His cornerstones through:

- Isolation (David in the field)
- Accusation (Joseph in the prison)
- Affliction (Job in suffering)
- Revelation (Moses in the desert)

ISOLATION – DAVID IN THE FIELD

"He chose David also his servant, and took him from the sheepfolds." —Psalm 78:70 (KJV)

Before David ever picked up a sword or wore a crown, he was isolated in the field—unseen, uninvited, and forgotten. While his brothers were training for battle, David was writing psalms in solitude and killing lions in silence. But God saw the field as His training ground for kings.

Isolation is not rejection—it's preparation.

In the field:

- You learn the sound of God's voice.
- You develop strength away from applause.
- You practice obedience with no audience.
- You become intimate with the anointing before you ever carry the assignment.

Isolation is where cornerstone leaders are born. It separates you from noise, distractions, and dependence on others—so that your foundation is rooted in God alone.

> **"When my father and my mother forsake me, then the Lord will take me up." —Psalm 27:10 (KJV)**

If you're in the field, you're not forgotten—you're being fortified.

ACCUSATION – JOSEPH IN THE PRISON

"Until the time that his word came: the word of the Lord tried him." —Psalm 105:19 (KJV)

Joseph was falsely accused, stripped of his coat, thrown in a pit, sold into slavery, and forgotten in prison. But even in the prison, the dream was alive. Accusation didn't destroy his destiny—it purified it.

Accusation is the furnace of the cornerstone.

It refines:

- Your motives.
- Your responses.
- Your character.
- Your dependency on God's vindication instead of man's validation.

Joseph didn't fight back with bitterness. He served faithfully, interpreted dreams, and trusted the process. His time in prison made him fit to carry the crown. Without accusation, Joseph would have been gifted but untested.

> **"No weapon that is formed against thee shall prosper; and every tongue that shall rise against thee in judgment thou shalt condemn…" —Isaiah 54:17 (KJV)**

If you've been falsely accused, don't panic—God is preparing to promote you through it.

AFFLICTION – JOB IN SUFFERING

> **"But he knoweth the way that I take: when he hath tried me, I shall come forth as gold." —Job 23:10 (KJV)**

Job lost everything—his wealth, his children, his health, and his friends. But he never lost his integrity. And through his suffering, Job came to know God in a deeper way than ever before.

Affliction is the pressure that reveals what your foundation is really made of.

For the cornerstone to hold weight, it must first be crushed.

- Job was faithful in the fire.
- He worshipped in his weeping.
- He held on when he had nothing left.

Affliction qualifies the cornerstone to comfort others, to lead with empathy, and to walk in authority that was earned in the furnace.

> "...after that ye have suffered a while, make you perfect, stablish, strengthen, settle you." —1 Peter 5:10 (KJV)

If you're suffering, trust this: affliction does not disqualify you—it refines you for greater responsibility.

REVELATION – MOSES IN THE DESERT

> "And the angel of the Lord appeared unto him in a flame of fire out of the midst of a bush..." —Exodus 3:2 (KJV)

Before Moses could lead others out of Egypt, he had to first be led into the desert of encounter. For forty years, he lived in obscurity. But it was in the burning bush moment that God revealed his true identity and assignment.

Revelation comes after everything else is stripped away.

- Moses was alone, but not abandoned.
- He wasn't looking for fire—but God sent it.
- He thought his purpose was over—but God reignited it.

Cornerstones carry revelation that births movements. But before God trusts them with strategy, He reveals His nature. Moses didn't just receive an assignment—he encountered God's holiness, God's name, and God's heart.

> "I am that I am… thus shalt thou say unto the children of Israel…" —Exodus 3:14 (KJV)

If you're in the desert, prepare—God is about to reveal Himself, and from that revelation, your mantle will rise.

THE MAKING OF A CORNERSTONE

You are not being punished. You are being positioned. The isolation, accusation, affliction, and revelation you've walked through have not been in vain. They are shaping you into a cornerstone—a weight-bearing, movement-carrying, revival-sustaining leader.

> "The stone which the builders refused is become the head stone of the corner. This is the Lord's doing; it is marvellous in our eyes." —Psalm 118:22–23 (KJV)

Each blow is not to break you but to prepare you.

YOU'RE NOT JUST A STONE—YOU'RE A STRUCTURAL ONE

Others may be part of the building, but cornerstones are essential. You're not extra. You're critical. This is why the enemy attacks you the way he does—because you're not just another stone. You are the one God is aligning others with.

Jesus was that cornerstone. And because He lives in you, you too are being built into something powerful (see **1 Peter 2:5–6**).

GOD ELEVATES WHAT MAN ELIMINATES

If you've been passed over, misused, overlooked, or criticized—take heart. The rejected stone is still God's chosen material.

You are being prepared to:

- Anchor ministries.
- Birth movements.
- Support families.
- Carry revival.
- Lead generations.

YOU ARE BEING PREPARED TO ANCHOR MINISTERS

"And I will fasten him as a nail in a sure place; and he shall be for a glorious throne to his father's house." —Isaiah 22:23 (KJV)

There is a kind of person God raises up in secret—not for the spotlight, but for the support beam. Not to be the loudest voice but to be the strongest foundation. You may not wear a title. You may not have a platform. But you are being shaped by God to anchor ministers.

You are the kind of person pastors call when they're weary.

You are the one intercessors lean on when the burden is heavy.

Pastor Dr. Claudine Benjamin

You are the one who holds leaders up when the fire gets fierce.

WHAT DOES IT MEAN TO BE AN ANCHOR?

An anchor is unseen beneath the surface, yet it keeps the whole ship from drifting. In the same way, spiritual anchors hold ministries steady:

- In times of spiritual warfare.
- During moral crisis.
- In seasons of emotional exhaustion.
- When leadership feels lonely or misunderstood.

You are being forged in fire, not for fame—but for faithfulness.

WHY YOU WERE REJECTED

Rejection often comes before promotion—not to destroy you, but to deepen you.

God hid you because He's building capacity within you.

You've been:

- Misunderstood because your wisdom exceeds your years.
- Isolated because God didn't want you contaminated.
- Silenced because your words carry the weight God is protecting.

But soon, He will plant you beside leaders—not to be elevated above them, but to stabilize what they carry.

BIBLICAL EXAMPLE: AARON AND HUR

> "But Moses' hands were heavy... and Aaron and Hur stayed up his hands... until the going down of the sun." —Exodus 17:12 (KJV)

Aaron and Hur weren't in the spotlight. They weren't holding the staff. But they held up the one who did. And because they stood firm, Israel won the battle.

Some are called to lead on the hill.

You are called to hold up the arms. That's not less important—it's often more powerful.

GOD IS MAKING YOU "A NAIL IN A SURE PLACE"

> "The glory of this latter house shall be greater..." —Haggai 2:9 (KJV)

In this hour, God is raising up:

- Spiritual midwives.
- Silent warriors.
- Watchmen on the wall.
- Intercessors who don't need a mic to shake hell.

You are not being overlooked—you are being overbuilt to carry the next wave of leaders.

God is making you a nail in a sure place—a person others will lean on when the shaking comes.

SIGNS YOU ARE AN ANCHOR IN THE MAKING

- You feel burdened for leaders more than for platforms.
- You pray in private more than you speak in public.
- You've endured rejection without growing bitter.
- You discern deeply but wait silently.
- You carry people in your spirit, even when they don't see you.

God is entrusting you with the hidden things—because you will protect the holy things.

YOU FEEL BURDENED FOR LEADERS MORE THAN FOR PLATFORMS

"I have set watchmen upon thy walls, O Jerusalem…" — Isaiah 62:6 (KJV)

While others chase microphones, some chase burdens. You may not seek attention, but you can't shake your intercession for pastors, prophets, and ministers. You're drawn to the weight they carry. You grieve when they fall. You fast when they're attacked. Why? Because you're not a spectator—you're an anchor.

You're not here to be seen—you're here to support. And your private burden is often more powerful than a public sermon.

CHARACTERISTICS OF THIS ANCHOR:

- You weep when others mock.
- You pray for preachers after the crowd leaves.

- You war in the spirit so others can minister in peace.

God burdens anchors first because they are trusted to carry what others drop.

YOU PRAY IN PRIVATE MORE THAN YOU SPEAK IN PUBLIC

"But thou, when thou prayest, enter into thy closet..." — Matthew 6:6 (KJV)

You may not be holding a microphone, but you are holding the line. While others are posting, performing, and platform-building—you're on your knees. You don't need a crowd to pray; the burden itself compels you.

Anchors live in the secret place:

- They intercede without applause.
- They break chains without credit.
- They birth breakthroughs others walk into.

You're not invisible to heaven. God hides those He honors. And your prayers are setting up battles others will win without even knowing why.

"The effectual fervent prayer of a righteous man availeth much." —James 5:16 (KJV)

Pastor Dr. Claudine Benjamin

YOU'VE ENDURED REJECTION WITHOUT GROWING BITTER

"He was despised and rejected of men…he opened not his mouth." —Isaiah 53:3,7 (KJV)

One of the greatest tests for spiritual anchors is rejection. You've been excluded from circles. Overlooked in rooms. Misunderstood by leaders. But instead of growing hard, you've stayed soft. That's the mark of someone God can trust.

Why were you rejected?

- To purify your motives.
- To keep you from pride.
- To draw you closer to the altar.
- To make you a safe place for others' pain.

Rejection didn't destroy you. It deepened you. And now, like Jesus—the Rejected Stone—you are being positioned as a cornerstone for others.

YOU DISCERN DEEPLY BUT WAIT SILENTLY

"To everything there is a season… a time to keep silence, and a time to speak." —Ecclesiastes 3:1, 7 (KJV)

You see what others miss. You hear what others ignore. You discern motives, atmospheres, and battles long before they manifest. But rather than rush to speak, you've learned to wait. To pray. To watch. That's maturity. That's wisdom. That's what anchors do.

Discerners who are also discreet are rare. But God is shaping you to:

- Be a prophetic protector, not a public exposer.
- Use revelation to intercede, not to impress.
- Speak when heaven says "speak"—and hold back when it says "not yet."

You don't just carry insight—you carry restraint. That's why He's calling you deeper.

YOU CARRY PEOPLE IN YOUR SPIRIT EVEN WHEN THEY DON'T SEE YOU

"Bear ye one another's burdens, and so fulfil the law of Christ." —Galatians 6:2 (KJV)

You carry names, faces, and burdens in your spirit. Not because they asked you to—but because the Spirit assigned you to. Even when they don't acknowledge you, you cover them.

You feel the weight of people's pain. You war on behalf of their destiny. You rejoice when they succeed and grieve when they drift. Why? Because you're not a spectator—you're a spiritual guardian.

This is the hidden ministry of the anchor:

- You cover what others expose.
- You pray for those who misunderstand you.
- You bear burdens without needing to be thanked.

Pastor Dr. Claudine Benjamin

And God says: *"Because you carry them, I will carry you."*

YOU'RE BEING TRUSTED WITH THE HIDDEN THINGS

"The secret of the Lord is with them that fear him…" —Psalm 25:14 (KJV)

Anchors are not built in public—they are forged in the dark. But what God does in hiding, He will honor in due time. You are being entrusted with secrets, assignments, and burdens that others cannot handle.

You are not rejected.
You are not invisible.
You are being refined for weight.

God is entrusting you with the hidden things—because you will protect the holy things.

BE STEADY. YOUR SEASON IS NEAR

The days of hiding are preparation. The fire you've been through is not to destroy—it's to forge an anchor. And soon, ministers will come to lean on you, churches will stabilize because of you, and the next move of God will stand secure because you were willing to be the stone that others passed over.

You are not a leftover. You are a load-bearer.

Let God finish building you.

You are being prepared to anchor ministers—and your assignment is sacred.

Your scars are not signs of shame—they're the proof of your strength.

THE CORNERSTONE HAS THE LAST WORD

The builders thought they were finished when they tossed the stone aside. But what they rejected, God resurrected. Jesus became the first and last Word.

Likewise, your story doesn't end where they dropped you. It ends at the cornerstone—where God places you in position, and the building cannot stand without you.

REFLECTION QUESTIONS

1. What areas of your life reveal God's preparation through pain?

2. Have you been resisting the chiseling process?

3. How do you now see yourself as a structural part of what God is building?

Chapter 6

Birth Movements

> "But God hath chosen the foolish things of the world to confound the wise…" —1 Corinthians 1:27 (KJV)

You may feel forgotten. Unseen. Passed over. But you are not being ignored by heaven. You are being incubated. Just as God used barren women in scripture to birth prophetic movements, so too is He preparing you—not for popularity, but for purpose.

REJECTION IS THE WOMB OF REVIVAL

Movements are not born in comfort; they're born in crushing.

- Joseph was rejected by his brothers but birthed a nation-saving movement.
- Moses was rejected by his people but led Israel out of Egypt.
- Jesus was "despised and rejected of men" but birthed the church.

You are not buried. You are planted. And what you birth will not be small—it will shake systems, liberate captives, and restore broken altars.

SIGNS YOU'RE ABOUT TO BIRTH A MOVEMENT

- You feel pregnant with something greater than yourself.
- You've been misjudged yet deeply burdened.
- Your private prayer life outweighs your public recognition.
- You can't "fit in" because you're called to break out.

Don't abort the mission because of opposition. Carry it full-term. Heaven is watching.

SUPPORT FAMILIES

"God setteth the solitary in families..." —Psalm 68:6 (KJV)

Some are called to preach revivals. Others are called to stabilize homes. You may not see yourself as a leader in the pulpit, but you are an anchor in the family.

Your prayers are upholding generations. Your love is breaking cycles. Your obedience is shifting bloodlines. You may have come from dysfunction, but you are being raised up to become a pillar of generational healing.

THE FAMILY YOU SUPPORT MAY BE YOUR OWN

- You intercede when no one else in the house knows how to pray.

- You teach children how to worship when their parents aren't watching.
- You steward the atmosphere of your home until it becomes a sanctuary.

You are not the leftover member of your family—you are the strategic stabilizer. God is using your rejection to make you a restorer of households.

BIBLICAL PICTURE: RUTH AND NAOMI

Ruth supported Naomi, not knowing she would become the great-grandmother of King David. You never know what you're preserving when you choose to stay, love, and serve.

CARRY REVIVAL

"The fire shall ever be burning upon the altar; it shall never go out." —Leviticus 6:13 (KJV)

Revival is not an event—it's a people.

It's not a schedule—it's a surrender.

And the people God chooses to carry revival are often the ones man rejected.

You are not being broken for no reason—you are being filled with holy oil. You are being prepared to carry the weight of glory without cracking. Not everyone can carry revival because revival is not light—it's costly.

WHAT REVIVAL CARRIERS LOOK LIKE

- You burn even when no one watches.
- You weep for souls others forget.
- You fast when others feast.
- You pray when others perform.
- You're more concerned with God's presence than your platform.

YOU'RE NOT WAITING FOR REVIVAL—YOU ARE REVIVAL

You may not have a mic, but you have a mantle.

You may not have a stage, but you carry a sound.

You may not have applause, but you have an assignment.

God uses rejected stones to ignite forgotten altars. Your tears have watered the soil. Your prayers have filled the bowls in heaven. Now get ready to carry fire.

DIVINE SELECTION IN THE MIDST OF HUMAN REJECTION

"Ye have not chosen me, but I have chosen you, and ordained you…" —John 15:16 (KJV)

One of the most powerful truths in the life of a believer is this: God chooses you, even when others reject you. The world may pass you over, but God never does. Human rejection cannot override divine election. God's call is not subject to popular opinion, majority vote, or social validation.

In fact, the ones God selects are often the ones others would never choose. But that's the beauty of grace—it qualifies the unqualified and selects the overlooked.

MAN LOOKS AT THE RESUME, GOD LOOKS AT THE HEART

When Samuel went to Jesse's house to anoint the next king of Israel, he was immediately drawn to Eliab—tall, impressive, and experienced. But God said no. One by one, Jesse's sons passed by, and one by one, they were rejected. Why? Because the one God had chosen wasn't even invited to the ceremony. David was out in the field, forgotten by his own father.

> **"Man looketh on the outward appearance, but the Lord looketh on the heart." (1 Samuel 16:7).**

Divine selection doesn't require man's spotlight—it only requires God's approval.

GOD SELECTS FOR DESTINY, NOT POPULARITY

When God chooses someone, He chooses based on purpose, not applause. He knows what's ahead and who's equipped to carry the weight of the calling. He chose Moses despite his speech problem. He chose Mary despite her youth. He chose Paul despite his past.

Your calling is not a mistake. Even if people cannot see your potential, God saw it before you were formed (see Jeremiah 1:5).

DIVINE SELECTION MAKES YOU A TARGET

The moment you are chosen by God, you become a threat to darkness and a mystery to people. David was anointed, but not everyone celebrated. His own brothers mocked him. Saul tried to kill him. But his oil still flowed. Anointing attracts both warfare and favor.

Don't be discouraged when people question your calling. Their doubt doesn't revoke God's decree.

REJECTION IS OFTEN A CONFIRMATION OF CALLING

Have you ever noticed that rejection often increases after you step into your calling? That's because divine selection causes spiritual resistance. But that resistance is often confirmation.

Jesus was baptized, affirmed by the Father, and immediately driven into the wilderness (see Matthew 4:1). Confirmation came—and then the confrontation. So, if you're being rejected, don't back down. You may be walking right in the center of your divine assignment.

YOU'RE NOT JUST CALLED—YOU'RE ORDAINED

John 15:16 is clear: **"I have chosen you, and ordained you..."** That word "ordained" means "appointed, placed, and positioned." You're not just called to exist—you're called to function. You've been placed by God to bear fruit that remains.

You're not random. You're not forgotten. You're not rejected by heaven. You are handpicked.

REFLECTION QUESTIONS

1. How has God affirmed your calling even when others did not?

2. Are you allowing rejection to define your worth—or are you standing on God's selection?

3. What would change in your life if you truly believed you are chosen?

Chapter 7

The Process of Becoming Foundational

"And hath made us kings and priests unto God and his Father…" —Revelation 1:6 (KJV)

"To whom coming, as unto a living stone, disallowed indeed of men, but chosen of God, and precious…" —1 Peter 2:4 (KJV)

Everyone wants to be used by God, but few want the process that shapes a person into a foundation. Being foundational means carrying weight, providing stability, and enduring pressure. And before God places a person in such a role, He takes them through fire, crushing, and refining.

FOUNDATIONS ARE FORGED IN FIRE

To become a foundation, you must first be formed. The process includes:

- Crushing: Like olives pressed for oil.
- Burning: Like gold refined by fire.
- Shaping: Like clay molded on the potter's wheel.

Pastor Dr. Claudine Benjamin

> **"If the foundations be destroyed, what can the righteous do?"**
> **—Psalm 11:3 (KJV)**

Before God builds on you, He builds within you. Before He places others in your life, He puts you through fire to make you strong, pure, and unshakable.

You may feel broken, hidden, or under intense pressure right now—but that's not a sign of rejection. That's the sign of formation.

All true foundations must be:

- Crushed like olives.
- Burned like gold.
- Shaped like clay.

Only then can you bear the weight of others.

CRUSHING – LIKE OLIVES PRESSED FOR OIL

> **"My soul is exceeding sorrowful, even unto death… and his sweat was as it were great drops of blood." —Matthew 26:38, Luke 22:44 (KJV)**

Olive oil is only released when the olive is crushed. Likewise, the anointing on your life is produced through pressure. This is not punishment—it's extraction.

God allows crushing to:

- Press out pride.

- Squeeze out self-will.
- Release the oil of obedience and anointing.

Even Jesus experienced Gethsemane—the olive press—before calvary. He was crushed in prayer before He was crowned in glory. And so must we be.

If you feel pressed:

- By trials.
- By betrayal.
- By unseen burdens.

Know this: oil is being produced.

> **"But we have this treasure in earthen vessels…" —2 Corinthians 4:7 (KJV)**

You are being crushed not to be destroyed but to be poured out.

BURNING – LIKE GOLD REFINED BY FIRE

> **"The trial of your faith… though it be tried with fire, might be found unto praise and honour and glory…" —1 Peter 1:7 (KJV)**

Gold doesn't fear fire—it requires it. The fire removes what cannot stay: impurity, mixture, excess. What remains is the valuable, unshakable core.

Pastor Dr. Claudine Benjamin

If you want to be a foundation in the kingdom, you must go through:

- Fiery trials.
- Testing seasons.
- Heat that reveals your true substance.

Fire will:

- Burn off distractions.
- Expose hidden motives.
- Refine your assignment.
- Produce spiritual authority.

When God allows fire, He is not destroying your value—He is revealing it.

> **"When thou walkest through the fire, thou shalt not be burned; neither shall the flame kindle upon thee." —Isaiah 43:2 (KJV)**

The fire that comes to purify you will become the same fire that protects and empowers you.

SHAPING – LIKE CLAY ON THE POTTER'S WHEEL

> **"O Lord, thou art our father; we are the clay, and thou our potter…" —Isaiah 64:8 (KJV)**

Being shaped by God is uncomfortable. It's not fast, and it's never convenient. But it's absolutely necessary.

The Potter puts His hands on your life:

- To stretch what was once rigid.
- To remove what doesn't belong.
- To smooth out what was once broken.

And sometimes—if the vessel becomes marred—He breaks and remakes it. Not because He's angry but because He sees greater use ahead.

> **"And the vessel that he made... was marred... so he made it again..." —Jeremiah 18:4 (KJV)**

If you feel like you're in a cycle:

- Spinning
- Uncertain
- Out of control

You may be on the wheel—in the hands of the Potter. Trust the process. He's shaping you to carry weight.

WHAT GOD FORMS, HE FOUNDS

God doesn't use shallow vessels to support deep movements. He uses forged foundations. Those who have:

- Endured the crushing.
- Survived the fire.
- Stayed on the wheel.

- And still worshipped through it all.

You may have been rejected by man—but you are being reinforced by heaven.

He is preparing you to:

- Anchor leaders.
- Stabilize ministries.
- Uphold revival.
- Father and mother generations.
- Carry lasting influence.

Because you're not just any stone—you are a cornerstone in the making.

"The stone which the builders refused is become the head stone of the corner. This is the Lord's doing; it is marvellous in our eyes." —Psalm 118:22–23 (KJV)

Let the crushing come.
Let the fire purify.
Let the shaping continue.
Because the foundation is almost ready.

Isaiah 48:10 says, **"I have chosen thee in the furnace of affliction."** Affliction doesn't destroy you—it proves you.

Every storm you've survived, every betrayal you've endured, and every tear you've cried is part of the shaping. God is building you for lasting impact.

REJECTION DEVELOPS THE RIGHT FOUNDATION

Stones that have been rejected are often the strongest because they have already endured impact. You've been dropped but not destroyed. Misjudged but not disqualified. God sees your strength even when others focus on your scars.

Your rejection is not random—it is God's way of proving your durability.

Just as a cornerstone must be solid to align the rest of the structure, so must you. You are the example others will follow. The leader others will lean on. The pattern others will replicate.

STABILITY REQUIRES STILLNESS

One of the greatest lessons of a foundation is stillness. It does not move when pressure comes. It holds its position. If you're going to be foundational, you must learn to be steady—even when attacked, misunderstood, or overlooked.

Psalm 46:10 says, **"Be still, and know that I am God…"** Foundational people don't react—they respond with wisdom, rooted in trust.

YOU'RE BEING BUILT INTO A LIVING HOUSE

1 Peter 2:5 calls believers **"lively stones."** This means you are part of a spiritual building—dynamic, growing, and essential. Each trial, each moment of crushing, is making you fit for God's structure.

Pastor Dr. Claudine Benjamin

You're not a temporary fixture. You're a permanent pillar. A vessel with legacy. A builder with eternal purpose.

FOUNDATION COMES BEFORE FRUITION

Everyone wants to bear fruit, but only what's rooted will remain. The deeper your foundation, the greater your capacity for fruit. God is preparing you for longevity, not just visibility. Don't despise the quiet, hidden seasons—they're the proof you're being planted, not buried.

REFLECTION QUESTIONS

1. What painful process has God used to shape your foundation?

2. Are you trying to bear fruit without developing roots?

3. How is God preparing you to be a cornerstone in someone else's life?

Chapter 8

You Were Rejected for a Reason

"But as for you, ye thought evil against me; but God meant it unto good…" —Genesis 50:20 (KJV)

"According as He hath chosen us in Him before the foundation of the world…" —Ephesians 1:4 (KJV)

It wasn't random. It wasn't accidental. It wasn't pointless. Your rejection—painful as it was—had purpose attached to it. You were rejected for a reason. It wasn't because you were unworthy; it was because you were marked for a greater assignment that couldn't fit where you were.

God never wastes pain, and He certainly never wastes rejection. What the enemy meant for evil, God is turning for your good. Every "no," every dismissal, every door that closed, and every circle that pushed you out—all of it is being used to prepare you for something greater.

REJECTION IS A SETUP FOR REDIRECTION

"You intended to harm me, but God intended it for good…"
—Genesis 50:20 (NIV)

Rejection stings. It confuses. It isolates. It whispers lies like, "You're not enough," or "You're unwanted." But through the lens of divine purpose, rejection is not your finish line—it's your launchpad. What looks like man closing a door is often God redirecting your destiny.

If you've been:

- Passed over
- Pushed aside
- Misjudged
- Mistreated

…take heart. You're in good company. Because every major figure God has used was first rejected—not to destroy them, but to redirect them.

REJECTION REDIRECTED DAVID TO THE THRONE

David was the son nobody counted. When the prophet came to anoint Israel's next king, David wasn't even invited to the meeting. His own father left him in the field.

But what man forgets, God remembers.

> **"Send and fetch him: for we will not sit down till he come hither." —1 Samuel 16:11 (KJV)**

God used that rejection to keep David in purity, humility, and preparation. The pasture wasn't punishment—it was positioning. David didn't need man's approval. He needed God's anointing. And rejection put him on the path toward it.

The throne he eventually sat on was not delayed—it was directed by rejection.

REJECTION REDIRECTED JOSEPH TO DESTINY

Joseph dreamed of greatness. But his brothers didn't applaud—they envied. They betrayed him, threw him in a pit, and sold him as a slave.

Rejection led him:

- To Potiphar's house (training ground).
- To prison (testing ground).
- To Pharaoh's palace (promotion ground).

> **"And the Lord was with Joseph, and he was a prosperous man..." —Genesis 39:2 (KJV)**

Joseph's pit was not the end. It was the first stop on the journey toward preserving nations.

Sometimes, betrayal is the vehicle God uses to get you to places loyalty never could.

REJECTION REDIRECTED JESUS TO THE CROSS—AND THE CROWN

"He is despised and rejected of men; a man of sorrows..." — Isaiah 53:3 (KJV)

Pastor Dr. Claudine Benjamin

Jesus was rejected by His hometown, betrayed by His disciple, falsely accused, mocked, and crucified. The religious leaders didn't recognize Him. The crowds chose Barabbas.

But every ounce of rejection led to the redemptive work of the cross. Man's refusal became heaven's revelation.

> **"The stone which the builders refused is become the head stone of the corner." —Psalm 118:22 (KJV)**

God used rejection to crown the Redeemer of the world. If the Son of God had to walk through rejection to fulfill purpose, so will you.

REJECTION PUSHES YOU INTO ROOMS YOU WOULDN'T ENTER OTHERWISE

Sometimes, rejection is God's mercy in disguise.

- That job you didn't get? It would have stunted your growth.
- That relationship that fell apart? It was pulling you away from your calling.
- That ministry you were shut out of? It wasn't your assignment.

> **"In all thy ways acknowledge him, and he shall direct thy paths." —Proverbs 3:6 (KJV)**

Rejection is often the closed door that keeps you on the right road. God shuts what won't serve you. He reroutes you toward what will release you.

REJECTION REFINES YOUR MOTIVES AND REDEFINES YOUR IDENTITY

Rejection:

- Strips your need for applause.
- Reveals who you are when no one is watching.
- Detaches your calling from people's opinions.
- Refines your hunger for God's affirmation alone.

When you've been rejected, and you still serve…
When you've been ignored, and you still worship…
When you've been pushed out, and you still pray…
You become unstoppable.

"Am I now trying to win the approval of human beings, or of God?" —Galatians 1:10 (NIV)

Rejection separates the performers from the pioneers. You're not performing for platforms—you're being prepared for purpose.

WHAT REJECTED YOU WILL REGRET IT

You are not being buried—you're being redirected.

The places that refused you will one day recognize you.

The people who doubted you will one day depend on your obedience.

Pastor Dr. Claudine Benjamin

The pain that shaped you is becoming the platform God will stand on.

Rejection wasn't the end. It was the detour to your beginning.

> **"This is the Lord's doing; it is marvellous in our eyes." — Psalm 118:23 (KJV)**

Joseph's brothers rejected him because of his dreams, not realizing that the dreamer they discarded would become their deliverer. The rejection led to a pit, which led to slavery, which led to a prison, which positioned him for the palace. Every stop along the way was a divine classroom.

You were rejected because you were being relocated to a space where your oil could flow freely. Some environments could not accommodate your calling. The rejection wasn't punishment—it was protection.

REJECTION TRAINS YOU FOR AUTHORITY

> **"Before I was afflicted I went astray: but now have I kept thy word." —Psalm 119:67 (KJV)**

Authority in the kingdom is never given cheaply. It's not earned by charisma, credentials, or applause—it's forged in pain, tested by rejection, and released through brokenness.

If you have been:

- Misunderstood
- Pushed aside

- Overlooked
- Lied on

…you may think you've been disqualified. But in truth, you're being qualified for spiritual authority. Rejection has become your classroom, and God is your teacher.

REJECTION KILLS THE NEED FOR VALIDATION

"Woe unto you, when all men shall speak well of you…" — **Luke 6:26 (KJV)**

God cannot entrust true authority to those who are addicted to applause. If you crave approval, you'll compromise under pressure. Rejection is the training ground where God detoxes you from the need to be liked.

Before David ruled a nation, he served in the shadows. Before Paul changed the world, he was isolated in Arabia. Before Jesus launched His public ministry, He endured thirty years of obscurity and thirty pieces of silver.

Rejection teaches you to need God's voice more than man's claps.

It replaces:

- Performance with purpose.
- Popularity with purity.
- Insecurity with identity.

You no longer live for acceptance—you live from acceptance.

Pastor Dr. Claudine Benjamin

REJECTION TESTS YOUR CHARACTER BEFORE YOU'RE ENTRUSTED WITH INFLUENCE

"He that is faithful in that which is least is faithful also in much…" —Luke 16:10 (KJV)

Authority without character is dangerous. So before God hands you people, He often allows you to face isolation, accusation, and disappointment. This is not cruelty—it's calibration.

Joseph couldn't govern Egypt until he learned humility in Potiphar's house and endurance in Pharaoh's prison. Rejection didn't derail him—it trained him. It made him fit to carry the weight of other people's dreams.

If God is building you to carry others, He must first crush everything in you that would destroy them.

REJECTION TEACHES YOU TO SERVE EVEN WHEN YOU'RE NOT SEEN

"And whatsoever ye do, do it heartily, as to the Lord, and not unto men;" —Colossians 3:23 (KJV)

Authority in the kingdom looks like servanthood, not spotlight.

Jesus washed feet. David served Saul. Joseph interpreted dreams in prison.

When you've been rejected, yet still:

- Serve
- Pray
- Worship
- Obey

...you develop the kind of heart God can trust with platforms, power, and people.

Rejection burns out entitlement and builds endurance.

It's God asking: *"Can I trust you to remain faithful when no one's watching?"*

REJECTION MAKES ROOM FOR REVELATION

"And he withdrew himself into the wilderness, and prayed."
—Luke 5:16 (KJV)

Authority is not just about managing people—it's about hearing God. Rejection often pushes us into the secret place where revelation flows freely.

Moses was rejected by Egypt and misunderstood by Israel. But in the wilderness, he received:

- The name of God.
- The law of God.
- The strategy for deliverance.

- The blueprints for tabernacle worship.

If he hadn't been rejected, he never would have ascended Sinai. Rejection doesn't just isolate you—it sanctifies your ears to hear God.

REJECTION PRODUCES COMPASSION AND INTEGRITY

"For we have not an high priest which cannot be touched with the feeling of our infirmities…" —Hebrews 4:15 (KJV)

Those who have been rejected know what it's like to hurt. And because of that, they lead differently. They don't lord authority over people—they carry it with compassion.

- You become slow to judge.
- Quick to forgive.
- Intentional with your words.
- Protective over the broken.

You've learned that pain doesn't disqualify—it prepares.

True authority doesn't crush people. It lifts them. Heals them. Restores them. And that's the kind of leader rejection produces.

REJECTION ISN'T JUST A TEST—IT'S A TRAINER

You're not being sidelined. You're being shaped.

You're not disqualified. You're being developed.

You're not forgotten. You're being formed for influence.

The Rejected Stone

> **"Humble yourselves therefore under the mighty hand of God, that he may exalt you in due time."** —1 Peter 5:6 (KJV)

When the time is right, you won't have to chase authority—it will rest on you because it knows you were forged in fire.

Rejection is not the end. It's the beginning of real leadership.

Before David ever wore a crown, he experienced rejection. His father didn't consider him worthy of the anointing (see 1 Samuel 16). Saul tried to kill him. Even his own men once spoke of stoning him (see 1 Samuel 30:6).

Yet through every painful moment, God was preparing David to shepherd a nation. Rejection matured him, broke pride, and taught him to depend entirely on God. Without rejection, David may have had charisma—but not character.

Rejection strips away entitlement and replaces it with endurance.

SOME WERE ASSIGNED TO REJECT YOU

There are people who were never meant to stay. Their purpose in your life was temporary, and their rejection of you was part of their assignment. Like Judas, they had to walk away. Like Saul, they had to fall. Like the builders in Psalm 118, they had to say "no" so God could say "yes."

This is difficult to grasp, but it is liberating. When you realize that certain rejections were necessary for your elevation, you stop mourning what left and start thanking God for what's coming.

Pastor Dr. Claudine Benjamin

YOU ARE NOT LESS—YOU ARE SET APART

To be chosen by God often means to be cut out of certain places. The stone that becomes the cornerstone is often carved out, trimmed, and refined in isolation.

You weren't rejected because you were less valuable. You were rejected because you were set apart for something that doesn't blend in with the crowd. You're not common—you're called.

GOD WILL USE THE SAME REJECTION TO RAISE YOU UP

In Acts 4:11, Peter boldly proclaimed that **"This is the stone which was set at nought of you builders, which is become the head of the corner." (KJV).** The very ones who rejected Jesus had to witness His exaltation. Likewise, God will let your enemies live long enough to see the glory rise on your life.

Your rejection was a required chapter in your redemption story. And your story is far from over.

REFLECTION QUESTIONS

1. Can you look back and see the divine hand behind your most painful rejection?

2. What assignment is your rejection preparing you for?

3. Have you made peace with being set apart?

Chapter 9

The Pain of Rejection and the Purpose Behind It

"For I reckon that the sufferings of this present time are not worthy to be compared with the glory which shall be revealed in us." —Romans 8:18 (KJV)

"He healeth the broken in heart, and bindeth up their wounds." —Psalm 147:3 (KJV)

Rejection hurts. There is no poetic way to disguise the sting of being pushed away, misunderstood, or cast aside. The pain of rejection cuts deeply because it hits where we are most vulnerable—our identity, our sense of worth, and our place in the world.

But rejection's pain is not where your story ends. It's often where your true story begins. Pain, in the hands of God, becomes purpose. And rejection, when surrendered to Christ, becomes a platform for glory.

Pastor Dr. Claudine Benjamin

REJECTION STRIKES THE CORE OF OUR IDENTITY

When we are rejected, especially by people we love or respect, it shakes us. We begin to question:

- Am I not good enough?
- What did I do wrong?
- Why wasn't I chosen?

Jesus understands this pain more than anyone. He was rejected by His own people: **"He came unto His own, and His own received Him not." (John 1:11).** He was betrayed by a disciple, denied by a friend, and abandoned at His crucifixion.

Yet through all that rejection, He never lost His identity. He knew who He was, and He knew who sent Him. When you know your identity in Christ, rejection can't rewrite your worth.

PAIN PUSHES YOU TOWARD PURPOSE

Sometimes, pain is the only thing that will move us. Rejection forces us to search deeper, cry harder, and lean into God more fully.

Hannah's pain in being barren drove her to a place of deep intercession. Elijah, after feeling rejected and hunted, had a divine encounter on Mount Horeb. Jesus, after rejection in Nazareth, moved on to Capernaum and performed mighty miracles.

Rejection isn't the end—it's a threshold to something greater. You are not being cast off. You are being called deeper.

GOD HEALS THE PAIN—BUT HE DOESN'T WASTE IT

Psalm 147:3 assures us that God heals broken hearts and binds up wounds. But He doesn't discard what broke us—He uses it.

Paul was rejected and stoned in cities that later became hubs of revival. Peter, after denying Christ, became a bold preacher. What once wounded them became part of their witness.

Your rejection carries a message. Your pain is someone else's hope. Your scars are someone else's sign of survival.

REJECTION BIRTHS INTIMACY WITH GOD

There is a closeness with God that only comes through suffering. Paul said, **"That I may know Him…and the fellowship of His sufferings." (Philippians 3:10).** When others walk away, God draws near.

The loneliness of rejection creates sacred space for God to minister, speak, and reveal destiny. It is in these moments you realize that the presence of God outweighs the approval of man.

PURPOSE DOESN'T ERASE PAIN—IT GIVES IT MEANING

You may still carry the ache of what happened. The words spoken. The door slammed. The betrayal endured. But when purpose shines through the cracks, it changes the narrative.

Jesus still bore the scars after the resurrection. The pain was real. But the purpose triumphed. His scars became proof of His victory, not a reminder of defeat. And so it shall be with you.

Pastor Dr. Claudine Benjamin

REFLECTION QUESTIONS

1. How has the pain of rejection shaped your prayer life or intimacy with God?

2. In what ways is God bringing purpose out of your pain?

3. What would it look like to use your rejection story to minister to others?

Chapter 10

Favor Finds the Forsaken

"When my father and my mother forsake me, then the Lord will take me up." —Psalm 27:10 (KJV)

"Surely, Lord, you bless the righteous; you surround them with your favor as with a shield." —Psalm 5:12 (NIV)

Forsaken. Forgotten. Abandoned. These are the emotions that often accompany rejection. When those who were supposed to love you walk away or fail to see your worth, it leaves a void. But the beautiful promise in God's Word is that when man forsakes you, favor finds you.

God's favor is not contingent on human acceptance. In fact, He often releases His favor in the very place you were rejected. Rejection may isolate you from people, but it never separates you from the favor of God.

REJECTED BY MAN, RECEIVED BY GOD

David knew what it meant to be forsaken. His father didn't even invite him to the anointing ceremony (see 1 Samuel 16). His brothers mocked him. Saul chased him. But through it all, God's favor followed him.

While others saw a shepherd, God saw a king. David testified, **"The Lord is my light and my salvation…" (Psalm 27:1).** His confidence came from knowing that though others left him, God lifted him.

Favor finds those the world overlooks.

FAVOR DOESN'T ALWAYS LOOK LIKE A PROMOTION—SOMETIMES IT'S PRESERVATION

We often expect favor to appear as elevation or applause. But sometimes, favor looks like protection. It was God's favor that kept Joseph alive when his brothers wanted to kill him. It was God's favor that preserved Moses in a basket floating down the Nile. It was favor that kept Daniel in the lion's den and the Hebrew boys in the fire.

If you're still standing after all you've endured, that's favor.

Even when you were in pits, prisons, or painful places—favor didn't forget you. It shielded you. Covered you. Sustained you.

THE FORSAKEN ARE OFTEN GOD'S FAVORITES

This is not about favoritism—it's about divine proximity. God draws near to the brokenhearted (see Psalm 34:18). He leans in close to the rejected. He whispers hope into the ears of those who've been pushed aside.

The Rejected Stone

Hagar was cast out into the desert, forsaken by Sarah, but God met her there and said, **"I see you"** (see Genesis 16:13). In the place of forsaking, Hagar discovered El Roi, the God who sees.

You are not invisible. You are not forgotten. Heaven sees you.

FAVOR WILL FIND YOU IN UNLIKELY PLACES

Joseph was in prison when Pharaoh's servants remembered his gift. Ruth was gathering leftover grain when Boaz noticed her. Esther was an orphan before she became a queen. These were not glamorous places—but they were divine locations for favor to locate them.

Wherever you are, however hidden you feel, favor knows your address.

GOD'S FAVOR HAS THE FINAL WORD

Man's rejection may be loud, but God's favor speaks louder. Psalm 30:5 says, **"In His favor is life..."** His favor brings healing, restoration, and access. It opens doors no one else can. It elevates in ways that human hands cannot orchestrate.

When favor finds you, it changes your name, your location, your status, and your future.

REFLECTION QUESTIONS

- Can you recall a time when God's favor sustained you in a low place?

Pastor Dr. Claudine Benjamin

- How can you shift your view of favor from promotion to preservation?

- Do you believe that God's favor will find you even in seasons of rejection?

Chapter 11

When Man Says No, But God Says Yes

"What shall we then say to these things? If God be for us, who can be against us?" —Romans 8:31 (KJV)

"Behold, I have set before thee an open door, and no man can shut it..." —Revelation 3:8 (KJV)

Man's "no" may feel final—but it never overrules God's "yes." Human opinion, policy, or prejudice can never cancel divine purpose. When man shuts the door, God can build a new one. When people disqualify you, God qualifies you. His yes is sovereign, irrevocable, and unstoppable.

YOU DON'T NEED MAN'S ENDORSEMENT TO FULFILL GOD'S ASSIGNMENT

Many are waiting for someone to affirm their calling before they walk in it. But throughout scripture, we see that God's yes doesn't require man's agreement.

Gideon was hiding when God called him a mighty man of valor.

Jeremiah tried to excuse himself because of his youth, but God said, **"Before I formed thee... I ordained thee." —Jeremiah 1:5 (KJV)**

Mary was an unmarried young girl, but God chose her to carry the Savior of the world.

Their qualifications didn't come from men—it came from God's "yes."

CLOSED DOORS ARE NOT ALWAYS CLOSED BY GOD

Sometimes, doors are shut by people—because of fear, pride, jealousy, or tradition. But just because man says no doesn't mean God did. Acts 5:38–39 reminds us that if something is of God, **"ye cannot overthrow it."**

When you've been rejected by systems or structures, trust that God has another door. And sometimes, He will create one that never existed before—just for you.

GOD'S YES OFTEN COMES IN THE MIDST OF REJECTION

Jesus didn't wait for the religious leaders to affirm Him. He walked in authority even as they tried to trap, test, and crucify Him. His "yes" from the Father empowered Him to endure every human "no."

When the woman with the alabaster box poured out her worship, the disciples rebuked her. But Jesus said, **"Let her alone; why trouble ye her? she hath wrought a good work on me."** (Mark

14:6). When man says "stop," God says "go." When man says "unqualified," God says "chosen."

THE "YES" OF GOD COMES WITH OPEN DOORS

In Revelation 3:8, Jesus speaks to the church at Philadelphia: **"I have set before thee an open door…"** This door was not opened by popularity, resources, or politics. It was opened by God Himself. And no man could shut it.

When God says yes, He backs it up with access. With anointing. With supernatural acceleration. You will walk into rooms you weren't invited to and sit at tables you didn't build—because God opened the door.

THE YES OF GOD IS YOUR SECURITY

When man says no, it can shake your confidence. But when God says yes, it becomes your anchor. You can walk boldly, speak confidently, and move forward without fear—because heaven has signed off on your destiny.

Romans 8:31 is a declaration: **"If God be for us, who can be against us?"** That's not a question. It's a victory cry.

REFLECTION QUESTIONS

1. What closed doors in your life might actually be opportunities for God to say yes?

2. How can you walk in confidence despite the "no" of man?

Pastor Dr. Claudine Benjamin

3. What areas of your life need to be re-submitted to God's yes today?

Chapter 12

The Stone That Broke the Mold

"Therefore thus saith the Lord GOD, Behold, I lay in Zion for a foundation a stone, a tried stone, a precious corner stone..."
—Isaiah 28:16 (KJV)

"And be not conformed to this world: but be ye transformed by the renewing of your mind..." —Romans 12:2 (KJV)

There are some stones that simply don't fit the mold. They don't conform to systems, traditions, or expectations. They're too bold, too unique, too pure, or too anointed to be molded by the hand of man. These are the stones that break the mold—often misunderstood, frequently rejected, but always chosen by God for something greater.

To break the mold means to disrupt the pattern—to challenge what is in order to make room for what must be. The stone that breaks the mold is the one that doesn't look like the others, act like the others, or move like the others—but is exactly what God needs for a new foundation.

Pastor Dr. Claudine Benjamin

BREAKING THE MOLD REQUIRES COURAGE

There is a cost to being different. Those who break the mold are rarely celebrated at first. Jesus didn't follow the traditions of the Pharisees—He healed on the Sabbath, spoke to Samaritans, and ate with sinners. They said He was a blasphemer, a troublemaker, a heretic. But He was the stone that would build a whole new covenant.

If you're going to break the mold, you must be willing to stand alone. You must resist the pressure to conform. God never called you to blend in—He called you to stand out.

GOD USES UNSHAPED STONES FOR UNSHAKABLE STRUCTURES

When Solomon built the temple, the stones were finished at the quarry so that no hammer or chisel was heard on the site (see 1 Kings 6:7). This is symbolic. God does His shaping in private—away from the noise of man's judgment.

The stone that breaks the mold may look awkward or imperfect at first, but it's being shaped by God's hand—not man's. You weren't called to be popular. You were called to be prophetic.

YOU CAN'T FIT INTO WHAT YOU WERE CALLED TO CHANGE

Many rejected stones struggle because they try to return to the mold that cast them out. They want acceptance. They want peace. But you cannot bring revival while seeking approval. The very mold that rejected you may be the system God sent you to reform.

Like Moses, who broke the mold of Egyptian royalty to become a deliverer…

Like Esther, who broke protocol to save a people…

Like John the Baptist, who lived in the wilderness rather than the temple courts…

…God has called you to be different—so that you can make a difference.

MOLD BREAKERS USHER IN NEW MOVEMENTS

Reformation always comes through those who refuse to be shaped by the old. When Jesus arrived, He said, **"Behold, I make all things new." (Revelation 21:5).** New wine requires new wineskins.

Your uniqueness isn't a flaw—it's an assignment. Your voice, your story, your gift is breaking ground for something that has never existed before.

WHAT THEY CAN'T LABEL, THEY OFTEN REJECT— UNTIL GOD ELEVATES IT

The religious leaders couldn't categorize Jesus, so they crucified Him. But the very stone they rejected became the foundation of salvation.

Don't allow man's discomfort with your uniqueness to silence your destiny. What breaks their mold fulfills God's master plan.

Pastor Dr. Claudine Benjamin

REFLECTION QUESTIONS

1. In what ways has your difference made you feel rejected?

2. Are you still trying to fit a mold God never called you to conform to?

3. What new thing might God be trying to build through your uniqueness?

Chapter 13

The Anointing That Cannot Be Ignored

> "But the LORD said unto Samuel, Look not on his countenance, or on the height of his stature…for man looketh on the outward appearance, but the LORD looketh on the heart." —1 Samuel 16:7 (KJV)

> "…the gifts and calling of God are without repentance." — Romans 11:29 (KJV)

There is a kind of anointing that cannot be silenced, hidden, or canceled. It's the anointing that remains even after rejection. The anointing that speaks louder than titles, credentials, or endorsements. It's the anointing that cannot be ignored.

When God places His hand on someone, no amount of criticism, sabotage, or delay can remove what He has ordained. Man may try to block it—but the oil still flows.

REJECTION DOESN'T REMOVE THE ANOINTING

David was anointed in private long before he was accepted publicly. Even after he was anointed, Saul hated him. His brothers belittled him. Yet David's anointing was undeniable.

What God placed on your life is still there—even after the betrayal, the disappointment, the failure. Rejection doesn't cancel the call—it often confirms it.

THE ANOINTING IS NOT DETERMINED BY POSITION

You may not have the platform, the microphone, or the spotlight—but if the anointing is on you, it will make room for you (see Proverbs 18:16). David was still tending sheep when the oil found him. Jesus was baptized in obscurity before He walked in authority.

Don't despise your wilderness. The oil often flows in secret places long before it's seen on public stages.

THE ANOINTING DISRUPTS COMFORT ZONES

The anointing exposes, shifts, and provokes. That's why it's often rejected at first. When Jesus read from Isaiah in the synagogue and declared the scripture fulfilled, the crowd marveled—then turned on Him (see Luke 4:18–29).

Your anointing will make some uncomfortable. That's because it calls people higher. It demands change. It disturbs tradition. But it is also the reason you cannot be ignored.

THE ANOINTING WORKS IN REJECTION'S AFTERMATH

Elijah ran from Jezebel and hid in a cave. But the anointing didn't lift. God met him there with a whisper. Paul was stoned, beaten, shipwrecked—but the anointing kept working. The rejected stone is often the most spiritually empowered.

Rejection may isolate you, but it cannot steal the oil.

YOUR ANOINTING WILL OUTLAST EVERY ATTACK

They may discredit your name. Disqualify your voice. Delay your assignment. But they cannot stop your oil.

The same Spirit that raised Christ from the dead lives in you. That power is not dependent on man's approval. The anointing is eternal, divinely given, and irreversible.

Let them reject. Let them walk away. Let them refuse to see. The oil is still on you—and it cannot be ignored forever.

REFLECTION QUESTIONS

1. Have you ever felt like your anointing was forgotten due to rejection?

2. Are you waiting for man's platform instead of walking in God's anointing?

3. What steps can you take to walk boldly in what God has already placed on you?

Chapter 14

Built by God, Not by Man

"Except the Lord build the house, they labour in vain that build it…" —Psalm 127:1 (KJV)

"For we are labourers together with God: ye are God's husbandry, ye are God's building." —1 Corinthians 3:9 (KJV)

When man builds, it can be impressive. When God builds, it is eternal. The stone that is rejected by human architects is often selected by the Divine Builder Himself. The difference? God builds based on destiny, not popularity. He doesn't look for polished, perfected, man-approved materials—He looks for surrendered vessels.

This chapter is a declaration to every rejected stone: You are being built by God, not by man.

MAN ASSEMBLES—BUT GOD ARCHITECTS

Humans assemble buildings. We erect platforms, construct systems, and draw blueprints. But the divine architect operates differently. God doesn't need man's tools—He builds with broken things, surrendered hearts, and hidden stones.

Moses was built in the wilderness. David was built in the pasture. Paul was built in isolation. Jesus was built in obscurity for thirty years before public ministry.

You may feel unseen, but heaven is hammering. You may feel discarded, but heaven is designing.

MAN CAN'T BUILD WHAT HE DIDN'T ORDAIN

One of the reasons you've been rejected is because man didn't recognize your blueprint. They couldn't place you because you don't fit their frame. Why? Because your structure was not designed by them.

You carry a heaven-born vision. That's why the old systems couldn't contain you. You're not their project—you're God's building.

1 Corinthians 3:9 reminds us that we are God's workmanship. He is the Master Builder. And what He builds—no man can tear down.

BUILT THROUGH PROCESS, NOT POPULARITY

God doesn't build overnight. He builds in stages:

- Foundation through faith.
- Structure through surrender.
- Endurance through trials.
- Glory through obedience.

The rejected stone is often shaped slowly. But what God builds through process will stand when storms come (see Matthew 7:24–25).

Let them rush their results. You endure the shaping. The house God is building in you will not fall.

DIVINE CONSTRUCTION OFTEN BEGINS IN DEMOLITION

Before Nehemiah rebuilt the wall, he had to inspect the ruins. Before God establishes, He sometimes has to strip everything that was built by flesh.

Don't panic when God starts removing things—relationships, platforms, crutches. That's not destruction. That's preparation. He's not breaking you—He's clearing the ground for what only He can build.

WHAT GOD BUILDS CANNOT BE STOPPED

When God ordains a building, it doesn't need man's permission. He will fund it, fill it, and finish it. Philippians 1:6 says, **"He which hath begun a good work in you will perform it…"**

The stone that was rejected by the builders has now become the cornerstone of God's house. You are not a mistake—you are His masterpiece.

Pastor Dr. Claudine Benjamin

REFLECTION QUESTIONS

1. Are you more focused on being built by man than by God?

2. What areas of your life is God trying to rebuild His way?

3. Can you trust the timing and method of God's construction in your life?

Chapter 15

When You Become What They Needed All Along

"Thou preparest a table before me in the presence of mine enemies…" —Psalm 23:5 (KJV)

"The stone which the builders refused is become the head stone of the corner. This is the Lord's doing; it is marvellous in our eyes." —Psalm 118:22–23 (KJV)

There is a full-circle moment that only God can orchestrate—when the stone that was once rejected becomes the very support others now lean on. When those who once cast you aside now come back needing your voice, your gift, your leadership, your oil.

This chapter is about the undeniable grace of God that takes the overlooked and turns them into the indispensable. When God elevates the rejected stone, He does so in such a way that even your enemies must acknowledge, "This is the Lord's doing."

Pastor Dr. Claudine Benjamin

YOUR VALUE DOESN'T CHANGE—THEIR VISION DOES

The stone never changed its nature. It was always valuable, always strong, always chosen. What changed? The builder's ability to recognize it.

When Joseph's brothers bowed before him, it wasn't because he became someone new. It was because God allowed them to finally see what was always there. *"You meant it for evil, but God meant it for good" (see Genesis 50:20).*

You don't need to change for people to value you. You just need to let God finish the process so they can no longer deny who you are.

THE SAME PEOPLE WHO REJECTED YOU MAY NEED YOU

This doesn't mean you walk in pride—it means you walk in purpose. David still served Saul, even though Saul tried to kill him. Joseph still fed the brothers who sold him. Jesus still forgave the very ones who crucified Him.

There is power in being the bigger vessel. When you bless those who cursed you, you don't shrink—you soar. And in doing so, you mirror Christ—the ultimate rejected stone who still saves those who denied Him.

GOD PREPARES TABLES, NOT TRAPS

Psalm 23:5 doesn't say He prepares a trap for your enemies. It says He prepares a table. Why? Because vindication in the kingdom looks like a blessing. Your elevation is not to prove them wrong—but to prove that God is righteous.

They will see you thrive, not to humiliate them, but so that they might repent and recognize God's hand on your life. This is why you must keep your heart clean—because how you handle elevation will determine whether you sustain it.

WHEN YOU BECOME A CORNERSTONE, OTHERS RELY ON YOU

What was once rejected is now a pillar. You are not just a survivor of rejection—you are now a support for others who feel the same.

- You become the counselor to the broken.
- The voice to the silenced.
- The door-opener to the shutout.

God takes the pain of your past and turns it into a platform of compassion and wisdom. Now, you are not just needed—you are nurturing.

FROM FORGOTTEN TO FOUNDATIONAL—BY GOD'S DESIGN

This is not about revenge—it's about redemption. The God who allowed the rejection is the same God who orchestrated the reunion. And now, like the stone in Psalm 118, you are positioned, purposed, and planted in a place no one expected.

This is the Lord's doing—and it is marvelous.

REFLECTION QUESTIONS

1. Are you prepared to become a blessing to those who once rejected you?

2. Can you recognize how God has preserved your heart for this moment?

3. What role are you now playing in the lives of people who once couldn't see your value?

Chapter 16

Restoration and Reinstatement

"And I will restore to you the years that the locust hath eaten…" —Joel 2:25 (KJV)

"After that ye have suffered a while, make you perfect, stablish, strengthen, settle you." —1 Peter 5:10 (KJV)

Rejection may take you through a season of loss—lost time, lost opportunities, lost confidence. But God is a Restorer. Not only does He heal the wound of rejection, but He restores what was lost and reinstates what was stolen.

The beauty of restoration in the kingdom is that it doesn't just bring you back to where you were—it advances you beyond where you would have been if you were never rejected.

RESTORATION BEGINS WITH INTERNAL HEALING

Before God restores things around you, He starts within you. Rejection wounds the soul. It leaves marks of shame, bitterness, and insecurity. But Psalm 147:3 promises, **"He healeth the broken in heart, and bindeth up their wounds."**

God's restoration starts in the place of pain. It speaks to your identity and affirms that you were never forgotten. You were always chosen.

When you are healed inwardly, you stop chasing validation externally. Restoration rewrites the inner narrative.

GOD RESTORES TIME—NOT JUST THINGS

Joel 2:25 speaks specifically of time: **"I will restore to you the years..."** Only God can redeem the time that feels wasted. Rejection might have delayed you, but it didn't derail you.

In the divine economy, what was stolen is returned with interest. You'll gain wisdom, favor, influence, and clarity in ways that would not have come without the rejection.

He is the God who restores speed, redeems purpose, and reinstates destiny.

REINSTATEMENT IS GOD'S PUBLIC VINDICATION

Restoration is often private, but reinstatement is public. It's when God places you back into position—not just healed but honored.

- Joseph was reinstated in Egypt as ruler after being cast aside.

- Job received double after his trial.

- Peter was reinstated by Jesus after denying Him three times.

Reinstatement means God places you back on the path of your assignment—stronger, wiser, and more anointed.

YOU DON'T HAVE TO FIGHT FOR IT—GOD WILL DO IT

In Isaiah 61:7, God says, **"For your shame ye shall have double..."** This is not something you strive for—it's something God gives. Restoration and reinstatement are acts of divine grace, not human effort.

You don't have to manipulate doors open. You don't have to prove your worth. You only need to remain faithful. God will handle your return.

REINSTATED TO LEAD, NOT JUST BELONG

When God restores and reinstates, He does so with purpose. He doesn't just bring you back in—He puts you at the head. You become a voice for others, a model of grace, and a carrier of breakthrough.

You were rejected, but now you're reinstated as a pillar. And what once felt like ruin becomes the platform for revival.

REFLECTION QUESTIONS

1. What areas of your life is God restoring right now?

2. Can you identify how rejection prepared you for leadership after restoration?

3. Are you ready to receive public reinstatement with humility and purpose?

Chapter 17

A Seat at the Table You Were Shut Out From

"Thou preparest a table before me in the presence of mine enemies…" —Psalm 23:5 (KJV)

"He raiseth up the poor out of the dust… to set them among princes…" —1 Samuel 2:8 (KJV)

There's a powerful moment in every rejected stone's journey—the moment God sets a table in front of those who once shut the door. This isn't about revenge—it's about vindication, validation, and visible elevation.

The very place where you were denied a seat is the place God will bring you back—not as a guest, but as a key voice.

YOU WERE NEVER MEANT TO BEG FOR A SEAT

So many spend years trying to prove they belong—auditioning for approval, altering themselves to fit a mold, or fighting for scraps of attention. But in God's kingdom, you don't beg for a seat—He builds you one.

The rejection of man is often God's way of saying, *"That's not your table. I'm preparing one with your name on it."*

Mephibosheth was forgotten and living in Lodabar, but David remembered him and brought him to the king's table (see 2 Samuel 9). His condition didn't disqualify him—his covenant gave him access.

You don't need to qualify. You need to remain in covenant.

GOD PREPARES THE TABLE IN THE PRESENCE OF YOUR CRITICS

Psalm 23:5 is not accidental. God doesn't prepare the table away from your enemies—He does it in front of them. Why? Because He wants to make it clear: This is My doing, not theirs.

They said you were unqualified. They laughed at your dream. They shut the door. But now they're watching you feast in the favor of God. And they'll have to admit—this isn't promotion from man. It's the product of grace.

YOU'RE NOT SITTING AT THEIR TABLE—YOU'RE SITTING AT HIS

Don't mistake this moment as a return to man-made systems. You're not being invited back into their circle—you're being seated in God's presence.

Luke 14:10 says, **"Friend, go up higher…"** When God brings you forward, no one can push you back.

The table you now sit at is not powered by politics, popularity, or position—it is sustained by divine purpose.

YOU'RE AT THE TABLE TO SERVE, NOT TO GLOAT

God's elevation is always missional. When He places you at the table, it's not to flaunt your favor—it's to fulfill your function.

Joseph didn't punish his brothers—he fed them. David didn't kill Saul when he had the chance—he honored him. Jesus didn't destroy His accusers—He died for them.

The table is not for proving your enemies wrong—it's for proving God right.

THE TABLE IS A PLATFORM FOR GENERATIONAL BLESSING

When you take your rightful seat, it's not just for you—it's for everyone coming after you. Your restoration, your reinstatement, your elevation—it's creating a seat for others who've been shut out.

You are the doorway others will walk through. And the rejected stone becomes the table-builder for the rejected generation.

REFLECTION QUESTIONS

1. What tables has God prepared for you in this season?

2. How can you serve others from your new seat instead of seeking validation?

Pastor Dr. Claudine Benjamin

3. What generational impact can your place at the table create?

Chapter 18

Rebuilding With Rejected Stones

"Ye also, as lively stones, are built up a spiritual house…" —1 Peter 2:5 (KJV)

"The stone which the builders refused is become the head stone of the corner." —Psalm 118:22 (KJV)

There's something powerful about how God works with the rejected. He doesn't discard what man throws away—He gathers it, redeems it, and uses it to build something new. God is not just restoring rejected stones—He's rebuilding with them.

The world looks for polished pieces; God seeks the broken. Man wants what looks perfect; God desires what's been purified through fire. The rejected stones that others overlooked are the very ones God is using to raise up a house that carries His glory.

GOD IS RAISING A NEW HOUSE WITH BROKEN PIECES

In 1 Peter 2:5, believers are called **"lively stones"**—living, chosen, and placed with purpose. These stones aren't flawless—they are full of testimony. They were once cast aside, but now they've become the foundation of something holy.

Every scar, every rejection, every "no" that tried to bury you has now become mortar in the walls of a new spiritual house.

You are not just being restored—you are becoming a builder with what was broken.

THE REJECTED KNOW HOW TO CARRY THE WEIGHT

When God builds with rejected stones, He builds something that lasts. Why? Because they know how to carry pain, persevere through pressure, and stand in places where others collapse.

- You've been weathered. You've been pressed. But now you've been chosen to support others.
- You are the mentor to the ones looking for direction.
- You are the intercessor for the ones still bleeding.
- You are the voice for the ones still voiceless.

REJECTED STONES BECOME RELIABLE ONES

"To whom coming, as unto a living stone, disallowed indeed of men, but chosen of God, and precious." —1 Peter 2:4 (KJV)

You've been through the storm. You've endured the pressure. You've walked through the fire and the silence, the betrayal and the breaking. But none of it was wasted.

The pain didn't disqualify you—it qualified you.

The weathering didn't wear you out—it made you weatherproof.

You weren't just rejected—you were reinforced.

Now, God is raising you up—not as a decoration, but as a foundation. Not as a performer but as a pillar.

You are now becoming what others can lean on.

YOU ARE THE MENTOR TO THE ONES LOOKING FOR DIRECTION

"That the aged men be sober, grave, temperate, sound in faith, in charity, in patience." —Titus 2:2 (KJV)

You've been through what others are just now facing.
You've learned to walk with God in the dark.
You've discovered how to listen when heaven is silent.
Now, God is calling you to be a guide.
Not from a place of superiority—but from survival.
You don't just teach—you testify.
You don't just advise—you empathize.
You don't just speak truth—you embody it.
Your scars are someone else's map to healing.
Your wisdom is their road back to purpose.
You are the voice that says, *"I've been there—and I'm still standing."*

Pastor Dr. Claudine Benjamin

YOU ARE THE INTERCESSOR FOR THE ONES STILL BLEEDING

"And the Lord turned the captivity of Job, when he prayed for his friends…" —Job 42:10 (KJV)

Some are still bleeding from what you've already survived.
Some are still bound by what God has already broken off of you.
And now you're not just a survivor—you're an intercessor.
You don't pray shallow prayers. You pray with groans.
With tears.
With memory.
With fire.
You war on behalf of those who are too weary to war for themselves. You may not be on a stage, but you're on your face.

You may not be public, but your prayers are piercing heaven and shifting atmospheres. Because reliable stones don't need applause to keep standing. They know who they are—and they know what they carry.

YOU ARE THE VOICE FOR THE ONES STILL VOICELESS

"Open thy mouth for the dumb in the cause of all such as are appointed to destruction." —Proverbs 31:8 (KJV)

There was a time you had no voice. No one listened. No one saw your pain. But now you've found your strength—and you are becoming an advocate.

You don't just speak up—you stand up.
You defend the broken.

You speak truth in hard places.
You echo heaven on earth.
And your voice has weight because it was forged in silence.

> **"The Lord God hath given me the tongue of the learned, that I should know how to speak a word in season to him that is weary:" —Isaiah 50:4 (KJV)**

Now, others are finding their voice through your obedience.

YOU ARE STABLE BECAUSE YOU'VE BEEN SHAKEN

> **"after that ye have suffered a while, make you perfect, stablish, strengthen, settle you." —1 Peter 5:10 (KJV)**

You've been through storms that would have collapsed others.
You've endured seasons that tried to steal your mind, your worship, your faith.
But now—you are settled.
You've been shaken, but now you're strong.
You've been rejected, but now you're rooted.

You've become:

- A refuge for others.
- A covering for the weak.
- A stabilizer in chaos.
- A builder in broken places.

You are the stone others ignored—but now you are the stone others lean on.

Pastor Dr. Claudine Benjamin

YOU'VE BEEN WEATHERED FOR A REASON

"The stone which the builders rejected is become the head of the corner." —Psalm 118:22 (KJV)

You weren't cast aside to be forgotten.
You were cast aside to be set apart.
God saw what others missed: a foundation stone.

So now, rise.

- Rise into your identity.
- Rise into your assignment.
- Rise into your reliability.

You are not just standing—you are supporting.
You are not just surviving—you are sustaining others.

Rejected stones become reliable ones. And reliable ones become revival carriers.

GOD DOESN'T JUST REUSE—HE REPURPOSES

This isn't just about reusing old materials—it's about transforming them. When God rebuilds with rejected stones, He upgrades their purpose. What was once simply stone becomes a sanctuary.

Rahab was rejected by society, but she became a part of Jesus' lineage. The woman at the well was avoided by others, but she became a citywide evangelist. Peter denied Christ, but he became the rock of the early church.

God takes what's been cast aside and gives it eternal purpose.

IT TAKES REJECTED STONES TO REACH REJECTED PEOPLE

God's house must be built with compassion. That's why He chooses rejected stones—because only those who have been broken can truly understand how to help the broken.

You've been through what they're going through. You've walked the same path of silence, shame, and scorn. And now your story is the bridge that leads others home.

Isaiah 61:4 says, **"And they shall build the old wastes, they shall raise up the former desolations…"** You are one of "they." The rebuilders. The restorers. The rejected who became repairers.

HEAVEN'S BLUEPRINT REQUIRES EARTH'S CASTAWAYS

God's kingdom is not built with celebrity—it's built with humility. Not with platform, but with purity. And so, He calls the rejected to become pillars in His temple (see Revelation 3:12).

You may have been thrown away by man, but in God's blueprint, you were always essential. The house He's building now will not crumble—because it's made with stones that have already survived every storm.

Pastor Dr. Claudine Benjamin

REFLECTION QUESTIONS

1. What part of your rejection story can be used to help build others?

2. How has your pain equipped you to be a pillar in God's house?

3. Are you willing to let God use your scars to construct something sacred?

Chapter 19

Satan's Counterfeit Doors

"There is a way which seemeth right unto a man, but the end thereof are the ways of death." —Proverbs 14:12 (KJV)

"The thief cometh not, but for to steal, and to kill, and to destroy..." —John 10:10 (KJV)

Just as God opens doors for the rejected stone to rise into purpose, the enemy works overtime to offer counterfeit doors—opportunities that mimic divine doors but lead to destruction. These doors are baited traps designed to pull you off course by preying on your wounds from rejection.

When you've been rejected, you crave belonging, affirmation, and visibility. Satan knows this. That's why his counterfeit doors often look good, feel right, and sound attractive—but their end is emptiness.

NOT EVERY OPEN DOOR IS FROM GOD

Revelation 3:8 tells us that only God opens doors no man can shut. But the enemy opens doors too—doors of distraction, compromise, and deception.

- A platform that elevates ego, not calling.
- A relationship that feeds flesh, not faith.
- A shortcut that bypasses process for popularity.

If the door costs your integrity, your peace, or your purpose—it's not God's.

COUNTERFEIT DOORS SPEAK TO WOUNDED PLACES

The enemy offered Jesus a counterfeit door in the wilderness—**"If thou be the Son of God, command that these stones be made bread." (Matthew 4:3)**. But Jesus didn't need to prove what heaven had already declared.

Likewise, Satan will offer you quick validation to satisfy deep rejection. But don't bite. What looks like a breakthrough may be bondage in disguise.

Be careful of doors that offer exposure but require you to dim your light, dilute your message, or defile your spirit.

DISCERNMENT GUARDS YOUR DESTINY

Hebrews 5:14 says that spiritual maturity comes through having senses trained to discern good and evil. Rejected stones need sharpened discernment because not every offer is from the One who chose you.

Before you walk through any door, ask:

- Does this door lead me closer to Christ?
- Does it require me to compromise?

- Will it produce fruit or fame?

Discernment is your spiritual filter. Use it, or deception will use you.

COUNTERFEIT DOORS LEAD TO DELAYED DESTINY

Many anointed people have walked through counterfeit doors and found themselves stuck—delayed by decisions they thought were divine.

Saul stepped through a door of disobedience by offering a sacrifice he wasn't called to give. He lost his kingdom. Samson followed the door of lust and lost his strength. Judas walked through greed's door and lost his soul.

One wrong door can cost years. Pray before you walk.

GOD'S DOOR WILL WAIT—SATAN'S DOOR WILL PRESSURE

God doesn't rush destiny. Satan does. God's doors are peace-filled. Satan's doors are fear-based and time-pressured. If it's laced with fear, shame, or pride—don't enter.

God's door may come later—but it will come with favor, fruit, and fire. Don't settle for a counterfeit when heaven has the real thing prepared for you.

Pastor Dr. Claudine Benjamin

REFLECTION QUESTIONS

1. Have you ever walked through a door that looked right but ended in regret?

2. How can you increase your spiritual discernment before making decisions?

3. Are you willing to wait for God's door, even if the enemy offers something sooner?

Chapter 20

Maintaining Access Through Worship and Warfare

"Enter into His gates with thanksgiving, and into His courts with praise: be thankful unto Him, and bless His name." — **Psalm 100:4 (KJV)**

"For the weapons of our warfare are not carnal, but mighty through God to the pulling down of strong holds." —**2 Corinthians 10:4 (KJV)**

Rejection does not just lead to restoration—it leads to access. Once God opens the door and sets the rejected stone in place, the enemy's next strategy is not to shut the door again—it is to distract you from staying inside. That's why it is not enough to walk through the open door of purpose; you must learn how to maintain access through ongoing worship and warfare.

Worship keeps you connected to the heart of God. Warfare keeps you equipped to resist the attacks of the enemy. Together, they are your spiritual rhythm—your key to remaining in the place God has planted you.

ACCESS MUST BE PROTECTED

Just because you've been granted access doesn't mean it will be easy to stay in the room. Satan doesn't mind you getting in—as long as he can push you out. He will use discouragement, division, deception, and distraction to make you question whether you belong.

But access must be guarded. Like Nehemiah rebuilding the wall, you must hold the sword in one hand and the bricks in the other (see Nehemiah 4:17). You build and battle. You worship and war.

WORSHIP IS YOUR WEAPON OF ATMOSPHERE

Worship isn't just a slow song—it's a spiritual strategy. It creates an atmosphere where God dwells. Psalm 22:3 says, **"Thou art holy, O thou that inhabitest the praises of Israel."**

When you worship:

- Confusion breaks.
- Clarity comes.
- Strongholds fall.
- Heaven invades your space.

Rejected stones must learn to become worshiping warriors. Worship is your reminder that you're still chosen, still covered, and still called.

WARFARE IS REQUIRED TO KEEP WHAT GOD GAVE

Paul told Timothy, **"Fight the good fight of faith…" (1 Timothy 6:12).** Why? Because elevation attracts warfare. Reinstatement invites resistance. The oil may have qualified you, but warfare trains you to keep it.

You're not just fighting for a title—you're fighting to keep your peace, your purpose, your posture, and your promise.

Spiritual warfare includes:

- Prayer
- Fasting
- The Word of God
- Discernment
- Declaring truth aloud
- Casting down imaginations (see 2 Corinthians 10:5)

Your greatest fight isn't with people—it's with the systems of thought that try to push you out of your rightful place.

ACCESS IS MAINTAINED THROUGH HUMILITY

Worship brings you low. It reminds you that the One who opened the door is the only One who can keep you there. Pride makes you vulnerable. But worship anchors your heart in humility.

Satan lost his place in heaven because he lost his humility. Judas lost his place in the ministry because he lost his reverence. Don't let pride poison the access God has given.

Pastor Dr. Claudine Benjamin

Stay low. Stay grateful. Stay surrendered.

LET PRAISE BE YOUR POSTURE AND WARFARE BE YOUR RHYTHM

When the walls of Jericho fell, it wasn't through weapons—it was through worship. When Paul and Silas were imprisoned, they didn't fight—they sang (see Acts 16:25–26). And the chains broke.

Praise is not a reaction to victory—it is a provocation of victory. The enemy cannot withstand a worshiper who knows how to war in the spirit.

When rejection tries to creep back in—worship.
When doubt whispers again—war with the Word.
When the room feels too big for you—lift your hands and remind the atmosphere who gave you the key.

REFLECTION QUESTIONS

1. Are you daily maintaining your spiritual access through worship and the Word?

2. How can you better balance rest and resistance in your current season?

3. What weapons of warfare has God given you that you need to sharpen again?

Chapter 21

The Door of the Final Hour

"Behold, I stand at the door, and knock: if any man hear my voice, and open the door, I will come in to him…" — Revelation 3:20 (KJV)

"Watch therefore, for ye know neither the day nor the hour wherein the Son of man cometh." —Matthew 25:13 (KJV)

Every story of rejection leads to a choice. Every restoration points to a decision. And every opportunity extended by God leads to one final and eternal reality: there is a door that only matters if it is entered in time—the door of salvation, the door of the final hour.

The journey of the rejected stone does not end with applause or achievement—it ends with alignment—alignment with God's eternal plan. This chapter is an urgent call not just to rejoice in being restored but to be ready. Because no matter how far you've come, there's one door that must never be missed: the door of the kingdom.

Pastor Dr. Claudine Benjamin

THE FINAL DOOR IS NOT JUST FOR THE REJECTED—IT'S FOR THE READY

Jesus stands at the door and knocks (see Revelation 3:20), but He does not force His way in. There comes a time when the knocking ceases, and the decision must already be made.

Rejection in this life is painful—but rejection by heaven is eternal. That's why your restored place on earth must be anchored in your secure place in eternity.

Don't just build here. Be sure your name is written there.

THE WISE VIRGINS WERE PREPARED

In Matthew 25, Jesus tells a sobering parable. Ten virgins awaited the bridegroom, but only five brought enough oil. When the door to the wedding feast was opened, the five wise ones went in, and the rest were shut out.

This is not just about oil—it's about readiness. Being chosen, being anointed, being once included is not enough—you must be ready when He comes.

Let the rejection you've experienced draw you closer to Christ, not just to calling. Don't miss the final door while celebrating all the doors He opened along the way.

THE FINAL HOUR REQUIRES URGENCY

We are not just in a season—we are in a prophetic hour. Time is accelerating. Signs are unfolding. Jesus is returning—not as the rejected stone, but as the ruling King.

There's no time to waste:

- No time to stay in bitterness.
- No time to remain stuck in cycles of shame.
- No time to postpone obedience.

You were rejected for a reason—but you are being redeemed for a mission. That mission is not just to sit at tables but to call others into the ark of safety before the door closes.

JESUS—THE STONE, THE DOOR, AND THE KING

On this journey, we have seen Jesus as the rejected stone. But He is also the door itself (see John 10:9). He is the entry point, the access, the passage into life. And in the final hour, He will be the one opening and closing the eternal gate.

The question is no longer, *"Will they accept me?"* but *"Am I ready for Him?"*

Rejection may have marked your past—but readiness must mark your future.

Pastor Dr. Claudine Benjamin

THE DOOR IS CLOSING—BUT IT'S STILL OPEN FOR NOW

There is still time to walk through. Still time to say yes. Still time to repent, return, and realign. But one day, the door will shut—just like in Noah's day. And when it does, it will be too late to knock.

Let every rejection push you toward Jesus. Let every open door on earth remind you of the greater door in heaven. And let your life declare to the world: I may have been rejected, but I walked through the only door that truly matters.

REFLECTION QUESTIONS

1. Have you secured your relationship with Christ, the true Door?

2. Are you helping others prepare for the final hour?

3. What distractions are keeping you from focusing on eternity?

Scripture Reference Index

(Grouped by theme for clarity and usability)

THE REJECTED STONE – PROPHETIC FOUNDATION

- Psalm 118:22
- Matthew 21:42
- Acts 4:11
- Isaiah 28:16
- 1 Peter 2:4–6

REJECTION AND DIVINE PURPOSE

- Genesis 50:20
- Jeremiah 1:5
- Romans 8:28
- 1 Samuel 16:7
- John 1:11
- Isaiah 53:3
- Luke 4:18–29

RESTORATION AND REINSTATEMENT

- Joel 2:25
- 1 Peter 5:10
- Job 42:10
- 2 Samuel 9

- Isaiah 61:7

DIVINE FAVOR IN REJECTION

- Psalm 27:10
- Psalm 5:12
- Genesis 39:21
- Luke 1:28
- Revelation 3:8

ANOINTING AND SPIRITUAL IDENTITY

- Romans 11:29
- 1 Samuel 16:12–13
- Isaiah 61:1
- Philippians 1:6
- 2 Corinthians 1:21–22

SPIRITUAL WARFARE AND ENDURANCE

- Psalm 100:4
- 2 Corinthians 10:4–5
- Ephesians 6:10–18
- 1 Timothy 6:12
- Hebrews 5:14
- Acts 16:25–26

ETERNAL READINESS AND FINAL DOORS

- Revelation 3:20
- John 10:9

- Matthew 25:1–13
- Revelation 21:5
- Matthew 24:44
- 1 Thessalonians 5:2

Conclusion

From Rejection to Royalty

The stone that was once cast aside has now become the cornerstone. This is not just a prophetic word—it is your personal testimony.

Rejection was never the end of your story. It was the beginning of your revealing. Every dismissal, every betrayal, every overlooked season was part of God's divine construction plan. The hands of men may have tossed you aside, but the hand of God picked you up, refined you, shaped you, and placed you exactly where you were always meant to be.

You are not defined by who walked away. You are not labeled by who couldn't see your worth. Your identity is not tied to man's rejection—but to God's selection.

This book has traced the path from being discarded to being destined:

- From the pain of being rejected
- To the process of being refined
- To the power of being restored

- And now, to the purpose of being positioned.

You are the stone God is building with. A living stone in His house (see 1 Peter 2:5). And He is not finished with you yet. Every chapter of your rejection has prepared you for this—your moment to rise, your season to lead, your time to stand.

Let the story of Christ—the ultimate rejected stone—anchor your hope. He was despised, beaten, and crucified. But He rose, victorious, as the Chief Cornerstone of salvation. And now, through Him, you too rise in resurrection power.

As you close this book, do not walk away with just inspiration. Walk away with revelation:

- You were rejected for a reason.
- You are now being restored with purpose.
- And you are called to help rebuild a generation.

Let your life be the proof that what man refuses, God redeems.

Let your story echo through generations:

"This is the Lord's doing; it is marvelous in our eyes." — Psalm 118:23

DECLARATION: I AM THE STONE HE CHOSE

I declare today that I am not forgotten.
I am not a mistake. I am not disqualified.
I am the stone that the builders rejected—
But God has chosen me for such a time as this.

I am not defined by man's opinion,
I am anchored in God's purpose.
Every scar tells a story of survival,
And every season of silence was God shaping me in secret.
I rise in boldness.
I stand in authority.
I walk through open doors with confidence,
Knowing I was created to be a cornerstone, not a castaway.
I will no longer beg for places I was never meant to fit.
I will no longer shrink to make others comfortable.
I am aligned with heaven's design.
I am a living stone in the Master Builder's hand.
This is my time to build, to bless, to break barriers.
I am chosen. I am placed. I am the stone He will use.
In Jesus' name. Amen.

CLOSING PRAYER

Heavenly Father,
Thank You for seeing what others missed. Thank You for loving what others left behind. You are the God who gathers the broken pieces and builds with them. You are the One who turns rejection into redemption. Lord, I surrender every wound, every word, every wall I've built from the pain of being rejected. Heal me, shape me, and place me where I belong—according to Your perfect will. Give me discernment to recognize counterfeit doors, wisdom to walk in humility, and courage to stand where others once said I didn't belong. Use my life as proof that You still restore. That You still elevate the rejected. That You still use the foolish things to confound the wise. May I never forget that Christ—the Rejected Stone—became the Cornerstone of my salvation. And now, through

Him, I am complete, I am called, and I am confident. In Jesus' name I pray. Amen.

www.ingramcontent.com/pod-product-compliance
Lightning Source LLC
Chambersburg PA
CBHW050833160426
43192CB00010B/2003